Introduction

Christmas has actually constantly been a favored holiday for Christians worldwide. It is a wonderful time for gift-giving and household get-togethers. The people entailed, in the biblical story, are interesting as well as they seem the just one seeking the promised Messiah. Over the centuries considering that Jesus was born in Bethlehem, extra and extra false characters have actually been included to the Christmas tradition.

There is no Santa Clause, Elves, Rudolph, Grinch, Snowmen, Trees, Holly, Ornaments or Mistletoe in the Bible tale of the birth of Christ. Charlie Brown and Snoopy were not there. The marketing of Christmas, with billions of bucks spent on presents that are not required, for people you do not such as, with money you don't have, has actually subdued the real factor of Jesus birth.

I hope here to reestablish the viewers to the genuine individualities that witness Jesus initially coming. These are the one included by Matthew as well as Luke in the Gospel accounts of Jesus' birth. People like:

Gabriel-The Angel sent out from God to introduce the coming of Messiah

Mary-The young mother of Jesus Joseph-The stepfather that elevated

Jesus

The Innkeeper-Unknown by name as well as oft-maligned The Shepherds-Those that were searching for His coming

Isaiah-The prophet that informed Israel exactly how to identify the good king

The Wise Men-Who followed the celebrity to locate the King Herod-The wicked incorrect king of Judah

Simeon-Who awaited the Consolation of Israel Anna-The old prophetess who offered in the Temple

Their stories inform us a lot concerning the political as well as spiritual times into which Jesus was birthed. We can gain from them that we are to live our lives, thinking God will constantly achieve His will. We need to live expecting His look anytime, and "when you think not."

These are their tales.

Chapter One
What the Angel Said

Every Christmas we listen to "Hark the Herald Angels Sing" as well as "Angels we have actually listened to on high, swiftly singing O'er the level." But according to Dr. Ed Leake and also the writer's self-study, angels do not sing. We have actually feminized these effective warrior beings to the factor that we no longer understand their goal and also their relevance.

Angels are effective spiritual beings produced by God to be His messengers to as well as guards of God's last production, guy. The Angels are not restricted to the real world that we know. They can transcend time and also room in their solution to God. They are mighty and also constantly described in the masculine type in the Bible. Not at all like the visuals above however more like a warrior. God also utilizes angels to communicate the satisfaction of special occasions to man.

In the scripture according to Luke, God sent out the Angel Gabriel with some unique information for all humankind. What the angel said on these three celebrations is really important to us, also in the 21st century.

The very first message delivered by Gabriel was offered to a Jewish priest as he used and prayed incense in the Temple. Zacharias and his spouse Elizabeth were childless as well as well up in years. They were praying for a kid when Gabriel showed up as well as claimed: "Fear not, thy prayer is listened to."

Luke 1:11 -13 "And there showed up unto him an angel of the Lord standing on the appropriate side of the altar of scent. When Zacharias saw, and

him, he was troubled, and also worry fell upon him. But the angel stated unto him, Fear not, Zacharias: for thy prayer is listened to: and also thy wife

Elisabeth shall bear thee a child, and also thou shalt call his name, John."
What a gorgeous point for us to recognize. God hears our prayers. The almighty God who created the universe and all that is in it cares sufficient concerning us to hear our prayers and also answer them.
Psalms 144:3 "LORD, what is guy, that thou takest understanding of him! or the kid of man, that thou makest account of him!"
When we call; He hears us when we sob; He hears us when we commend Him as well, he hears us. He also answers us when we do not think, as He did Zacharias. God took his speech away till John was born due to the fact that he did not think the message from the angel. Despite the fact that he questioned, God answered his prayer.
6 months later on Gabriel was sent out to a young woman in the city of Nazareth with one more message from God. When the angel appeared, this female was engaged to a man called Joseph as well as was in the purification duration showing her virginity. She may have been wishing God to send the Messiah, not knowing that God would choose her for that particular purpose.
Luke 1:26 -28 "And in the 6th month the angel Gabriel was sent out from God unto a city of Galilee, named Nazareth, To a virgin upheld to a guy whose name was Joseph, of your home of David; and the virgin's name was Mary. And also the angel can be found in unto her, and stated, Hail, thou that art very favoured, the Lord is with thee: honored art thou among females."
God informs us, that we are extremely preferred. In Jeremiah 1:5 God states.
" Before I developed thee in the belly I recognized thee." God also cares and also understands

about us before we are birthed. We are all very preferred. In this verse, God proclaims His love for us. He wants only the very best for each and every of His youngsters. We are, extremely favored.
God showed His love for male when He, nine months later on, sent the angel to a tiny team of shepherds. As they rested at camp one evening, the glory of the Lord brightened the sky and the Angel of the Lord, (probably Gabriel), showed up to a band of guards. They were the ones trying to find the coming Messiah. Not the Pharisee's, Scribes, Priests or Rulers. Just a few of God's faithful

followers.
Luke 2: 9-10 "And, lo, the angel of the Lord bumped into them, and the magnificence of the Lord shone round regarding them: as well as they were sore scared. And the angel stated unto them, Fear not: for, behold, I bring you great tidings of great delight, which shall be to all individuals."
God wants to bring each people excellent tidings and terrific pleasure. What far better message than for God to declare that He had actually offered a method for us to invest endless time with Him in paradise. God knows what we need as well as has actually promised to provide all our requirement. The greatest requirement of guy is a Saviour. We are alienated from God because of our sin, as well as without a Saviour, we have no expect going to Heaven. That is not all the angel said. Below was one more declaration in each of these 3 messages.
God does not want us to be afraid. Not Him. Not our scenario. Not the wickedness of this globe. Not our future in the world or after fatality.
Luke 2:11 -14 "For unto you is born this particular day in the city of David a Saviour, which is Christ the Lord. As well as this shall be an indication unto you; Ye will locate the babe covered in swaddling clothing, lying in a manger. As well as instantly there was with the angel a multitude of the incredible host applauding God, as well as saying. Magnificence to God in the highest possible, and also in the world peace, goodwill toward men."

God sent His kid to be born of a virgin as well as come to be a male, live a clean, sinless life so that He might crave our transgressions on the cross of Calvary thirty-three years later. Jesus met the demand of Holy God to ensure that we might have eternal life. We can "fear not" due to what Jesus did on Calvary.
No one can satisfy the righteous needs to be acceptable to a Holy God. We should be holy, perfect as well as sinless, but none of us are. That's why we require a Saviour.
Romans 3:10 "As it is written, there is none exemplary, no, not one:"
Most of us are worthy of God's wrath for our disobedience to His rules.
Romans 6:23 "For the wages of wrong is death, however the gift of God is immortality with Jesus Christ our Lord."
Death, as used here, implies timeless separation from God. Spiritual death, in a real hell. We made it through our sinning.

John 3:16 -18 "For God so loved the world, that he provided his only begotten Son, that whosoever believeth in him should not perish, but have long lasting life. For God sent out not his Son right into the globe to condemn the globe; however that the world with him could be saved. He that believeth on him is not condemned: yet he that believeth not is condemned currently since he hath not believed in the name of the only begotten Son of God."

That very first Christmas day God sent His son, Jesus, to earth as the Saviour, the greatest present that God could give to man. We are condemned, currently. Through Jesus, we can be saved from God's wrath as well as get His tidings of excellent happiness. And also have no concern of the rage to come. Jesus pertained to save those who would certainly think. He pertained to bring mercy for all our sins, past, future and also existing. He still conserves today. Just believe that Jesus passed away in your location and also you as well can have immortality. Simply ask Him to conserve you.

Chapter Two
Stepfather

Matthew and also Luke tell the true story of a Saviours birth. We understand concerning Mary, the mom of Jesus. We know concerning the Angels that came. We know the shepherds. And also the wise men. We have actually become aware of Simeon and Anna. And also even about evil Herod. What do we know concerning Jesus' stepfather, Joseph?

We think Mary was rather young. Historical works suggest that Joseph was a possibly much older, for he was "the Carpenter." In the land of a unrestricted rocks and also few trees, where houses were built of rock, that might suggest that he was more of a stonemason than a timber crafter. Still, there's much we do not know.

Matthew 1:18 "Now the birth of Jesus Christ was on this sensible: When as his mommy Mary was upheld to Joseph prior to they integrated, she was discovered with kid of the Holy Ghost."

Formerly as videotaped in Luke, Mary was informed that she would certainly have a youngster, of the Holy Ghost.

Understanding, the impossibilities of this Mary asked, "how can this.

be?"

She traveled from Nazareth to Hebron, a distance of regarding 115 miles to review this matter with a family member named Elizabeth, that was wed to a clergyman called Zacharias. At this time Elizabeth was six months expecting with a boy, John, that would be called the Baptist. An additional miraculous maternity. When Mary returned to Nazareth after John's birth, she was in her 4th or fifth month as well as starting to show when she informed Joseph the tale of Gabriel's look.

Embraced (Engaged).

Under Hebrew law, the duration of betrothal produced what the equivalent of a civil agreement of marital relationship to be properly complied with by a religious. Engagement was essentially marital relationship and might only be broken off by an official expense of divorcement. The bride did not go at when to her hubby's house. He needed time to prepare an area for his spouse. She required time for prep work as well as to soften the pain of separating from her friends, or maybe in component from her parents. An interval would elapse, that might last from a number of weeks or months to also as for much is an entire year. This moment range demonstrated proof of her pureness.

Mary was upheld Joseph, called "a just man" in Mathew 1:19 was a righteous guy. Mary's maternity need to have created him excellent distress because Hebrew legislation required one of 2 solutions. The unfaithful bride-to-be, in addition to the angering guy, were both to be taken outside the city and also publically stoned to fatality. Or the hubby might give her an expense of divorcement which informed everybody "this female is not my other half and I am not her partner." The bride-to-be was, then went back to her dad's home, and all wedding plans terminated.

Dream Number One (Get Married to Mary).

It is while Joseph believed on these points as well as duke it outed them in his sleep the angel appeared to him in a dream with a message from God.

Matthew 1:19 -21 "Then Joseph her hubby, being a just man, as well as not happy to make her a public instance, was minded to put her away privily. However while he thought on these points, behold, the angel of the.

Lord appeared unto him in a dream, stating, Joseph, thou son of David, are afraid not to take unto thee Mary thy spouse: for that which is developed in her is of the Holy Ghost. As well as she shall come up with a child, and also thou shalt call his name JESUS: for he will conserve his people from their transgressions.".

Joseph having thought Angel's message in the dream continued to take Mary as his other half.

When Caesar declared that all the world ought to be tired, Joseph took Mary as well as traveled to the community of Bethlehem to sign up for the taxes because Joseph as well as Mary were both descendants of King David.

Luke tape-records the events in Bethlehem. The birth of Jesus in the manger; The appearance of the Angels; The browse through of the Shepherds. Matthew recorded when the smart guys came, later, and with the aid of Herod's scribes, they venerated and located Jesus in Joseph's residence in Bethlehem. The sensible males, being advised in a desire, returned to their land without going back to Herod in Jerusalem.

Dream Number Two (Flee to Egypt)-- Age 2.

Matthew 2:13 -18 "And when they were departed, look at, the angel of the Lord appeareth to Joseph in a desire, claiming, Arise, and take the child and his mother, and take off into Egypt, and be thou below until I bring thee word: for Herod will seek the little one to ruin him. When he developed, he took the young child and his mommy by evening, as well as departed into Egypt: And existed until the fatality of Herod: that it could be met which was spoken of the Lord by the prophet, stating, Out of Egypt have I called my son. Then Herod, when he saw that he was buffooned of the smart guys, was surpassing wroth, as well as sent out forth, and also multitude all the children that remained in Bethlehem, and also in all the shores thereof, from

2 years of ages and under, according to the time which he had vigilantly made inquiries of the sensible guys. After that was met that which was spoken by Jeremy the prophet, claiming, In Rama was there a voice listened to, lamentation, and also weeping, and fantastic grieving, Rachel weeping for her children, and also would certainly not be comforted due to the fact that they are not.".

While God could have safeguarded his Son in Bethlehem, from the wrath of Herod, an angel of the Lord showed up to Joseph, in a dream, and regulated him to take off to Egypt.

Herod the Great, recognized for the growth of the Temple, was also among the most fierce and harsh kings ever before to rule over Israel. Herod was kept in mind for killing his 2 children as well as likewise his partner, so his order to slaughter the male children 2 years old and also under is in character with Herod the (not so) Great. So Joseph took his young household and also utilizing the wealth obtained from the Magi to finance their trip they took off to Egypt.

Dream Number 3 (Return to Israel)-- Age 4.

Matthew 2:19 -21 "But when Herod was dead, witness, an angel of the Lord appeareth in a dream to Joseph in Egypt, Saying, Arise, as well as take the young child and also his mommy, and enter into the land of Israel: for they are dead which sought the kid's life. As well as he occurred, and took the young child and also his mother, as well as came into the land of Israel.".

Joseph once more immediately complied with Gabriel's message and also took Mary and Jesus as well as returned to the land of Israel.

Dream Number 4 (Return to Nazareth).

Matthew 2:19 -23 "But when Herod was dead, witness, an angel of the Lord appeareth in a dream to Joseph in Egypt, Saying, Arise, and also take the child as well as his mommy, and also enter into the land of Israel: for they are dead which sought the child's life. As well as he occurred, and also took the young kid and his mom, and entered the land of Israel. But when he heard that Archelaus did rule in Judaea in the room of his daddy Herod, he hesitated to go thither: regardless of, being advised of God in a dream, he transformed aside into the components of Galilee And he came and also dwelt in a city called Nazareth: that it might be met which was spoken by the prophets; He will be called a Nazarene.".

When Herod died, of a pesky condition, in the same year that he had eliminated all the children, Caesar divided his kingdom among his 3 living boys. Archelaus got dominion over Jerusalem and Judah. History tells us that he was much more fierce and crueler that his father, Herod. He was not liked by the Jews, and also immediately upon his ascension slew 3,000 Jews in the Temple at the Passover.

Life in Nazareth.

Jesus matured in a phenomenal home. His step-father Joseph was understood for his saintliness of character as well as integrity of conduct (Matthew 7:11). He came from a commercial center class, being an architect-builder and also timber workman. He prepared as well as constructed residences, produced furniture as well as agricultural tools. In Nazareth, he appeared to have obtained, by his personality and market, to a special area of esteem and also efficiency as well as was called by the title 'The Carpenter." He appears to have actually lived long as well as left his substantial family members, when he died, to the care of his boy Jesus. (Jesus had four half-brothers as well as 2 half-sisters).

Jesus half-brothers were James, writer of the book of James, Joses,.

Judas, author of Jude, and also Simeon (Mark 6:3). Half-sisters Assia as well as Lydia as recognized in historic documents. They did not become followers up until after Jesus' rebirth.

Jesus at age twelve.

Luke 2:41 -49 "And when he was twelve years old, they went up to Jerusalem after the custom-made of the banquet. As well as when they had satisfied the days, as they returned, the kid Jesus tarried behind in Jerusalem; and also Joseph and also his mom understood not of it. They, expecting him to have actually been in the firm, went a day's trip; and also they sought him among their kinsfolk as well as colleague. And also when they discovered him not, they reversed once again to Jerusalem, seeking him. As well as it happened, that after three days they discovered him in the temple, sitting in the midst of the physicians, both hearing them, and asking concerns. As well as all that heard him were amazed at his understanding and also responses. And when they saw him, they were astonished: as well as his mom stated unto him, Son, why hast thou hence handled us? Behold, thy papa as well as I have actually sought thee sorrowing. As well as he claimed unto them, How is it that ye sought me? Wist ye not that I must have to do with my Father's service?".

After discussing Scripture with the found out scholars in Jerusalem, Jesus went back to Nazareth with his parents where he went through them and also boosted in wisdom and also stature as well as favor with God and also guy. Evidently, Joseph died at some time prior to Jesus started His earthly ministry. Some state Jesus had to do with 18 years of ages when Joseph passed away.

God sent His Son to begin His earthly life just as all human beings have actually done because Eve birth a kid to Adam. He laid aside His godly magnificence and.

power to end up being a defenseless infant, suffered via all the pains of growth right into teenage years as well as with all the pressures of the teenager years that we encountered. He learned from his earthly father and mom the routines of every day life with bros and also siblings. Without Sin.

In His grown-up life, He contended several enemies as well as unbelievers, yet without wrong. He faced the leaders and also spiritual leaders of His day concerning their wicked methods, yet without wrong. He was falsely implicated, completely beaten and tortured, yet without transgression.

Chapter Three
He Chose Me

Luke 2:19 "But Mary maintained all these points and also considered them in her heart."
In Genesis chapter 3 God promised that the seed of the female would certainly bruise the head, (a deadly injury) of the snake.
Genesis 3:14 -15 "And the LORD God stated unto the serpent, Because thouhast done this, thou art cursed most of all livestock, as well as over every monster of the area; upon thy belly shalt thou go, and also dirt shalt thou eat all the days of thy life: And I will put enmity between the and the female, and also in between thy seed and her seed; it will bruise thy head, as well as thou shalt bruise his heel."
This verse has the first pledge of a saviour in the Bible, as well as it occurs after Adam as well as Eve learnt more about wickedness and required to hear of God's love and strategy of redemption. God understood that man would certainly rebel versus His authority and the only method to remove guy's sin would cost Him the life of His only begotten and also sinless Son. He created Man as well as Woman anyway in spite of the high price.
From the day of Adam's rebellion, Satan has actually repeatedly attempted to break

the line from Adam to Jesus, the Saviour. He triggered the initial man born to kill his bro. He lead guy to end up being so wicked that God needed to damage the entire globe with a globally flooding. Only 8 individuals survived in an Ark

developed by Noah.
In Genesis twelve God selected a guy called Abram to be the dad of the guaranteed Messiah. Because, Abram, later on called Abraham, was to father the line leading via Isaac and also Jacob (Israel) to the Saviour, the Israelites came to be the most resented individuals on earth. Satan did not desire a Saviour to be born.
From generation to generation, Satan attempted to quit the line. He also looked for to have the Jews eliminated in the days of Moses. God opened up the Red Sea to save His people and also lead them right into a land of their very own.
God guaranteed David that the Messiah would be a descendant of his.
2 Samuel 7:17 -17 "But my mercy shall not leave far from him, as I took it from Saul, whom I put away before thee. And also thine residence and also thy kingdom will be established for in the past thee: thy throne shall be established permanently. According to all these words, and according to all this vision, so did Nathan talk unto David."
After David, there came a sequence of kings, some great, however primarily wicked. The last of which was Jeconiah (AKA: Jehoiachin, Jechonias, Coniah). Jeremiah calls him Coniah and records the judgment of God versus him and his offspring.
Jeremiah 22:29 -30 "O planet, planet, planet, hear the word of the LORD. Therefore saith the LORD, Write ye this man childless, a man that will not thrive in his days: for no guy of his seed will thrive, resting upon the throne of David, and also ruling anymore in Judah."
No descendant of Jehoiachin would certainly ever before remain on the throne of Israel.

According to Matthew, Joseph was a descendant of Jehoiachin. Was the line damaged or did God have another strategy from the beginning?
Matthew 1:7 -11 "And Solomon begat Roboam; as well as Roboam resulted in Abia; and Abia begat Asa; And Asa begat Josaphat; as well as Josaphat resulted in Joram; and Joram begat Ozias; And Ozias begat Joatham; as well as Joatham resulted in Achaz; and also Achaz begat Ezekias; And Ezekias begat Manasses; and also Manasses resulted in Amon; and Amon resulted in Josias; And Josias begat Jechonias and his brethren, regarding the moment they were

carried away to Babylon:"
The foreknowledge of God understood the plans of Satan to thwart the plan to provide His son, so God had a various plan initially. The plan of God entailed the seed of the lady (Genesis 3:15).
Luke provides us the family tree of Mary:
Luke 3:23 -31 "And Jesus himself began to be concerning thirty years of age, being (as was supposed) the kid of Joseph, which was the kid of Heli (Mary's daddy), Which was the kid of Matthat, which was the kid of Levi, which was the kid of Melchi, which was the son of Janna, which was the son of Joseph, Which was the child of Mattathias, which was the boy of Amos, which was the kid of Naum, which was the child of Esli, which was the kid of Nagge, Which was the child of Maath, which was the boy of Mattathias, which was the son of Semei, which was the child of Joseph, which was the kid of Juda, Which was the kid of Joanna, which was the kid of Rhesa, which was the son of Zorobabel, which was the son of Salathiel, which was the child of

Neri, Which was the kid of Melchi, which was the son of Addi, which was the boy of Cosam, which was the child of Elmodam, which was the boy of Emergency room, Which was the boy of Jose, which was the kid of Eliezer, which was the child of Jorim, which was the kid of Matthat, which was the son of Levi, Which was the son of Simeon, which was the child of Juda, which was the boy of Joseph, which was the child of Jonan, which was the kid of Eliakim, Which was the kid of Melea, which was the child of Menan, which was the son of Mattatha, which was the kid of Nathan, which was the son of David,"
Mary's line was through David's kid Nathan while Joseph's line was through the cursed family tree from David's kid Solomon.
Jesus deserved to rule Israel from Solomon and also the spiritual authority to be the Messiah Savoiur from Nathan.
God chose a girl to be the vessel in which He would provide His Son as a ransom money for the globe Adam offered to Satan when he willfully disobeyed God and also selected to be his very own god. Sin entered our globe in Eden, but redemption came at Calvary.
As Mary Fairchild observed, in her write-up "Meet Mary: Mother of Jesus," Mary was a simple slave of God, trusted God as well as obeyed His call.

Her dad, Heli had made a "ketubbah" contract with Joseph for the marriage of his daughter, Mary. The customized of Jesus' day was the bride would certainly choose her partner, and also the dad would certainly authorize the legal agreement. From the signing, the pair were lawfully married. Mary was like any kind of various other bride, delighted about her brand-new life, when the angel, Gabriel showed up.

Luke 1:29" And when she saw him, she was bothered at his stating, as well as cast in her mind what manner of salutation this need to be."

Fearful Mary asked what this greeting implied and was told that she

had been picked to be the mom of the long-promised Messiah. Every Jewish female in history has longed to be the one to bring to life God's assured redeemer and since choice was placed prior to her.

Not knowing exactly how God would certainly achieve this mirage to conserve her individuals, she faithfully placed her rely on God, equally as Esther had carried out in Persia years before. How the fertilization would happen or how Joseph would react she did not understand. Mary trusted the elegance of God to fulfill these obstacles.

Mary originated from a spiritual family, also her relative had actually married a priest, however she knew the shame of an unwed mom was ahead of her. Joseph can even terminate the marriage as well as have her stoned. Her submission to God's strategy would cost her a lot, yet she wanted to endure for a season in order that the globe would certainly obtain a saviour.

" God recognized that Mary was a lady of unusual stamina. She was the only human being to be with Jesus throughout his whole life-- from birth up until fatality." (Mary Fairchild).

Mary was young. She was poor and additionally a woman, every one of that made her unsuitable for solution to God according to contemporary Jewish teaching. God chooses according to His will as well as not man's demands. He had actually also consisted of 4 gentile females in the lineage of the Messiah.

Matthew 1:3 "And Judas resulted in Phares and Zara of Thamar; ...".

Matthew1:5" AndSalmonbegatBoozof Rachab; as well as Booz begat Obed of Ruth; ...".

Matthew 1:6 "David the king results in Solomon of her that had been the

partner of Urias;".
Mary gave birth to Jesus as her child boy as well as would enjoy Him die on the cross as her saviour. God knew she would voluntarily offer Him in this most important job due to the fact that of her belief. God sent his Son, born of a woman, the seed of a woman, to cost-free mankind from the penalty of sin. God checks out our loyalty as well as desire to serve Him, and also not our.

qualifications.
1 Corinthians 4:2 "Moreover it is called for in stewards, that a guy be discovered faithful.".
1 Corinthians 1:25 -29 "Be-cause the absurdity of God is smarter than guys; and also the weak point of God is more powerful than men. For ye see your calling, brethren, exactly how that few wise males after the flesh, very few mighty, not many noble, are called: But God hath picked the silly points of the globe to amaze the sensible; and also God hath selected the weak points of the globe to confuse the things which are mighty; And base things of the world, as well as points which are disliked, hath God selected, yea, and also points which are not, to bring to nought things that are: That no flesh must delight in his visibility.".
God chose a young, bad, however loyal female to use as the automobile to bring us His redemption with the blood of His only begotten Son, Jesus.
Mary would certainly be the one to light the candle lights in preparation of Seder: The Passover party aiming to the Lamb of God.
Just a woman can kindle the event lights. The rabbis have long instructed that without the lady to bring the light, the tale of redemption can not start. It was, too, that through a Jewish woman, God offered us the One that is the true Light of the globe (Jn. 8:12).
John 8:1 "Then talk Jesus again unto them, saying, I am the light of the globe: he that followeth me shall not stroll in darkness, however shall have the light of life.".

Chapter Four
Old Shep Learns about Christmas
Adapted from story by E . Marie DeGol

In a little community in Egypt, Old Shep, the sheepdog, scampered up the hill where he saw Old Barney existing under a tree relaxing his weary body and staring up into the skies. Since he was various in some way from any other donkey he had actually ever seen, Shep was curious concerning Barney. He viewed Barney forage and also consume alcohol water from the creek, and he was typically off by himself-- almost as if he didn't even recognize any of the various other pets were around. Old Barney had a mystical look concerning him, as well as Shep was getting anxious. He composed his mind that he would certainly come right out as well as ask Barney why he was satisfied and so quiet just being by himself.

When Barney saw Shep coming close to, he claimed and smiled, "Old Shep, what brings you here, until now far from your sheep?".

" It's you, Barney. Frankly, I'm anxious concerning you. Are you ill? I haven't seen you grazing with the others lately, as well as I concerned see if you are alright," was Shep's reply.

Barney claimed as well as laughed, "How extremely kind of you to be so worried regarding me, however you do not need to stress. I am extremely pleased, as well as I am never ever lonesome because I have numerous lovely memories to comfort me in my seniority. I mean I'm just a ridiculous, old donkey particularly around this time around of the year.".

Old Shep extended beside him, yawned and scratched his ear and then asked, "What do you suggest 'this time of the year'?".

Old Barney took a look at Shep with awe and addressed, "It's nearing Christmas

time. Really did not you know that?".
" No," said Old Shep, "What is Christmas? You understand just how foolish I am. I've invested all my life in this pasture doing nothing but view the lamb, as well as they know even much less than I do. They can not think on their own. I have to lead them to the turf.".

Old Barney understood everything about the sheep and just how they goofed about as though they were blind, however he couldn't understand Shep because he was not silly. He was the most intelligent sheepdog in town, but then Barney realized that Shep was also active watching out for the sheep that he didn't have time to discover anything else. Barney really did not respond to immediately, and Shep waited some time as well as firmly insisted that.
Barney, tell him concerning Christmas. Barney claimed to Shep, "I wouldn't intend to see you get into any type of difficulty by being so far from your sheep. Your master has to be worried about you. It's getting near sundown." Shep assured him that the other dogs were with the shepherd and that he had the evening to himself. He huddled beside Old Barney as well as listened.
" Many years ago in a community called Nazareth," Barney started, "I was standing in the marketplace waiting to be gotten. Numerous sellers existed, as well as I was examined over and also over, and I feared nobody would pick me since I was so young and also was never ridden. Lastly, a silent guy came up to me and also touched me ever so carefully and bought me. He led me to his, house and also tied me outside his woodworker store. He spoke gently to me as well as fed me fresh hay daily and made sure I constantly had lots of water. He was wed to a lovely young woman, and also I might see that she was with child. Every little thing was quiet as well as so relaxed until one day I heard them speaking about a mandate made by a vicious, unearthly king that everyone need to most likely to his hometown for federal government enrollment. Well, I really did not understand what all this indicated, yet I understood they were about to take me on my very first trip to a town called Bethlehem.
I didn't have any kind of suggestion where or exactly how much it was, yet I made sure my kind master would lead me. I additionally recognized that I was to carry the Gentle Lady and also I must not stop. I understood I would certainly have to be extra careful due to her condition.

as well as I began to fear that I may stumble and also terrify her. When I started out with her on my back, I experienced the strangest sensation. She felt ever so light, and also I was filled with such strength. I could not comprehend all of it.".

Old Shep's eyes widened with shock since he recognized how in contrast donkeys can be, yet Old Barney continued.

" Yes, it's true. I recognized my unique freight, and also I walked very delicately so as not to trigger her distress. They chatted tenderly backward and forward, and also my master kept asking his lady if she intended to relax awhile. Each time they stopped; to eat, they gave me fresh water and time to forage, but they never ever stuck around also long so I understood we need to hurry. After numerous days of travel, I might see that the Gentle Lady was getting tired as well as my master came to be extra anxious due to the fact that their quits were less constant. He maintained inquiring about her convenience, and she constantly guaranteed him that she was alright. I was much eased when I heard him state, 'We are nearing the Inn, my cherished. Try not to be afraid; we will certainly reach there in time.' I understood then that he suggested that she would deliver at the Inn. She murmured a number of times, and also he clasped her hand, and also I recognized she remained in much pain. I tried to go much faster and also made use of every ounce, of toughness I had to reach the Inn. It was nighttime when we ultimately arrived there, and also the Gentle Lady sighed with relief when my master knocked on the door of the Inn. The door opened up, as well as I listened to a voice state gruffly, 'I'm sorry, there's no space at the Inn,' as well as the door virtually knocked shut.".

Old Shep raised and also excitedly said, "Oh, Barney, exactly how unfortunate! What did they do?" Barney got to over to soothe Shep and proceeded.

" My master led us away from the Inn to a stable where the other pets, mostly lamb were birthed and cared for called Migdol Ader.".

He quietly told the keeper that his other half prepared to deliver as well as inquired if an edge could be provided for her. The caretaker nodded and also led us to a tiny vacant space. My master extremely carefully raised the Gentle Lady from my back, as well as he made a bed of hay for her. I vacated the way and also transformed my head and also cried. Quickly I heard the small cry of an infant, as well as I listened to the tender voice of my master claim, 'Rest currently, my better half, and also be glad, for your Son is born, as well as unto the world, a Saviour is given.'.

" Then he came by to me and also patted me as well as gave me fresh hay as well as.

water. Suddenly, a hush fell over the secure, as well as a radiant beam of light ruptured forth like the rays of the sunlight for a brilliant star radiated as well as came over the secure. My eyes were drawn toward the Child, and through my tear-dimmed eyes, I saw the Saviour. Back then I really did not comprehend what everything implied. It had not been up until regarding 2 years later on that I understood the full definition of that night.".

Old Shep's eyes were filled with tears, as well as he stretched out his paw to touch Old Barney who was additionally weeping. It was a beautiful tale that Barney informed Shep, however he still really did not recognize what Christmas was all about.

" But, Barney, what does all this concern Christmas?" he asked.

softly.

Old Barney trembled. The rips from his face and also continued. "As soon as the. Mild Lady was able to take a trip, I lugged her as well as the Baby to a residence they located in Bethlehem. One day as I was grazing-near your house, I saw 3 men approaching. They entered your house, and also I strolled over to the window and glimpsed in. I saw them kneel down before the Child, whose name was Jesus, to praise Him and also to offer their gifts of gold, incense, and myrrh. I knew they were the Wise Men regarding that I heard the people talking a lot. I additionally recognized then that this Baby, Jesus, was the King regarding who the entire community was speaking. They stated He would be born King of the Jews, and that He was the Messiah for who everyone was looking. He was sent! from God to conserve individuals from their transgressions.".

Old Shep cut off, "What is a transgression?".

Barney responded to, "Everything that is negative as well as incorrect. You understand, like disobeying your master as well as quarreling among each other and doing things you shouldn't.".

" Oh," said Shep, "I recognize what you indicate. I have actually been bad at times, but I attempt to be great.".

" Be that as it may," Barney responded, "Everyone misbehaves. That's why God sent His Son, this Baby Jesus. To offer His individuals Eternal Life.".

Shep stretched once more as well as damaged his ear and also was extremely puzzled. He claimed, "But, Barney, I still do not understand. I told you I am silly. I want to know just how I can be great constantly.".

Barney changed his weight to his side and also went on with his story. "When.

God developed the globe, He made whatever best. Jesus created everything; even you and also me, as well as all the other pets. But, He was lonesome, so He determined to produce man and woman, you know, individuals. God made them best as well as put them in an excellent garden, and told them they can consume anything they wanted except the fruit on one private tree. He informed them that if they consumed from that tree, they would eventually pass away. Well, Satan, the evil one, you recognize, the one that desires us to be bad, showed up in the form of a stunning serpent to the woman, Eve, as well as informed her that she would not pass away if she consumed from the tree, as well as he informed her to proceed and take a bite. Well, she did consume, and also the fruit was so tasty that she gave some to her husband, Adam. He assumed that given that she ate it and also didn't pass away, it would certainly be alright for him to consume it also, so, he, too, did eat. This was the first wrong due to the fact that they disobeyed God and also it made Him very angry. God then told them that since they sinned, they would pass away and the entire world, likewise, would certainly pass away. You see, if they would certainly not have eaten of the forbidden fruit and would certainly have obeyed God, the world would still be best, and people would certainly live forever. But, because of their wrong in the Garden, God is making the whole globe pay. Well, He saw that the people couldn't keep all His regulations, so He had to generate a far better method to save His people which He had created. He enjoyed them too much to see them pass away and also not be with Him. The only way God could have an ideal strategy was to give His very own Son up for His individuals. He was to take the sinner's place. Well, the people toenailed His Son to a wood cross, as well as he died there for everybody in the entire globe. His excellent Son took all the wrongs of the entire world and craved everyone to make sure that they might most likely to heaven when they die and to give them Eternal Life. Yet, after he was in the grave 3 days, He occurred and also went back to His Father, Who sent Him so He might become our door to the Father. All should make a serious decision.".

" What is that?" Shep asked excitedly.

" Everybody has to admit his wrongs in order to be forgiven and ask Jesus to find right into their heart and also do everything that Jesus asks," Barney answered.

Shep assumed for a minute and then shook his head and also claimed, "I'm just a pet; not a person. What concerning me? Besides, I do not believe I could do everything He asks. What if I forget and also do something wrong?".

That's why we require the Saviour, Jesus," answered Barney. "He becomes our helper, as well as with Him in our hearts, no one intends to do bad.

points. God made a promise that He would certainly never ever leave those who called upon Him and also allowed Him to enter their heart. And also, He likes us, as well, since He additionally developed us.

And did you know that He allowed Adam to give us a name? He called you 'pet dog,' and also he called me, 'donkey,' otherwise, we would certainly still be called 'animal.' He constantly provides for His very own. He provides for you via your master, doesn't he?" Barney asked.

" Oh, yes. He.must love me a lot due to the fact that I never go dehydrated or hungry.

Barney, just how do I obtain Jesus to live as well as come in my heart?" asked Shep.

" Simply by asking Him and also meaning it. He said He stands at the door of every heart as well as knocks as well as whoever opens the door and invites Him in will live forever with Him in heaven. This is what people call Eternal Life," Barney described.

Old Shep jumped up as well as checked into Barney's eyes in the moonlight as well as asked, "How can I ask? I do not understand what to claim. Oh, I do intend to go to paradise and live forever with Jesus and also all the various other good individuals, but I don't know what to state. Will you please aid me?"

Barney reached over to assure Shep and stated, "Just repeat after me these words, 'Dear Jesus, I love you.' That's right, bow your head as well as simply claim the very same words I am saying.' Barney went on, and Shep duplicated, "Thank you for loving me and for craving me. I regret my sins. Please forgive me and also please come into my heart as well as take control of my life as well as aid me to live for You. I ask this, in Your Holy Name. Amen.'

As quickly as Shep stated the "Amen" he rejoiced due to the fact that he was so pleased. He extremely solemnly stated to Barney,

" Thank you, Barney. I feel like a brand-new canine. I'm so satisfied. People are so fortunate to have actually received such an unspeakable Gift."

" How right, Old Shep," replied Barney, "If just they approve Him. Currently do you; understand about Christmas?"

" Yes, oh, yes, Barney. It's the birthday of the Baby Jesus. As well as I can now understand why you are so different from all the various other donkeys. You assisted to bring this Gift into the globe, as well as I am so lucky to have you as my close friend.

Thanks for informing me this stunning tale and also for assisting me to be a much better canine.
Look! Just how brilliant the celebrities are! They are the light of the evening. Aren't they stunning?" asked Old Shep.
" Yes, Old Shep, they are," answered Barney. You see the light of the evening, but I saw the Light of the World!"
With these words, Old Barney fell under a deep sleep, and also Old Shep crawled up across Barney's back as well as rose and closed his eyes and also licked the face of the most blessed donkey in the world.

Chapter Five
No Vacancy

New Jersey, 21st Century

A number of years ago we experienced one of the so-called "Noreaster" storms that frequent the East coastline of the United States. Generally, these tornados come up the coastline, disposing snow or moisten the coastal communities and after that drift to the right and blow themselves out in the North Atlantic. This, nonetheless, made a decision to move across the Delaware Bay as well as into South Jersey. The storm reduced trees, which pulled down high-voltage line and also blocked the roadways. After that, following day, the July sunlight appeared, as well as the temperature level increased into upper 90's. Without power for AIR CONDITIONING, cooking or lights and also aid 4 to 5 days away we were encouraged to secure the home and head west for shelter. We filled the colders with points that required refrigeration as well as headed throughout Pennsylvania towards my 90-year-old mommy's retired life home.

The plan was to drive a couple of hrs, then drop in a motel for the night. The first motel and the ones around everything revealed "No Vacancy" indicators. We went one more hr west to a leave with numerous significant resort chains. They all had No Vacancy. I tried the remainder location where all the motels had their contact number noted. No Vacancy's for thousands of miles.

Around 1:30 AM we got to Mother's and were welcomed with a cool home, soft bed as well as great fellowship. 5 days later on we had the ability to return house and also start the clean-up procedure.

Bethlehem, 1st Century

" Father, might I hang the 'no vacancy' sign currently? You rented the last room an hour ago, and also now you have actually just rented my room. There is no place left for anyone else to stay."

" I'm sorry my child, but you and also your sibling can oversleep the hay wagon tonight or for the next several nights.We requirement to make as several Denarii as we can throughout this time around of the census. Caesar might never ever call again for such a tax obligation enrollment, so we have to make as much cash as we can now."

" I am sorry sir, yet we are filled out. There is no more area in the inn, and my son was about to hang the no job indication. "

" But sir, I implore you to find an area for my bride-to-be and me to clean and rest off the dirt. We have been taking a trip from Nazareth to obtain below in time for the registration, and also she is excellent with child. The baby might come anytime now. Mary is very tired, so possibly we can rest in your lobby for a just bit."

" Jacob, can't you see this woman is expectant. We need to discover an area for her to remain."

" Yes Mama, but the Inn is full, all the spaces are taken, all the beds are crowded, there's no even more area for any person, anywhere."" Then locate someplace. Someplace exclusive where this girl might bring to life her baby."

" OK mama, I will certainly speak with the rabbis at Migdal Eder where they take care of the sacrificial lambs. Perhaps they will have a personal as well as clean area for Mary to give birth. They are both offspring of King David, from who the Messiah is ahead. So this kid might be the Promised One be born below in Bethlehem this very evening."

Micah5:2 -3" Butthou, Bethlehem.

Ephratah, thoughthoubelittleamongthe.

countless Judah, yet out of thee will he emerge unto me that is to be leader in Israel; whose goings forth have actually been from of old, from long lasting. 3Therefore will certainly he provide up, till the time that she which travaileth hath.generated: after that the residue of his brethren shall return unto the children of Israel.".

Micah 4:8 "And thou, O tower of the group, the strong hold of the little girl of Zion, unto thee shall it come, even the initial rule; the kingdom shall involve the little girl of Jerusalem.".

This tower was for monitoring the field of the sheep that were to be used in the sacrifices in the Temple at Jerusalem. According to the Mishnah, each birth of a lamb was checked out by the Rabbinic Sheppard and licensed "without place or acne" and also acceptable for sacrifice.

Delivering in the Migdal Eder would certainly be the perfect area for Jesus to be born considering that He was as John proclaimed "the Lamb of God that taketh away the sins of the globe." It likewise discusses exactly how the Shepherds recognized where to try to find the "Babe covered in swaddling garments" as newborn lambs were wrapped in swaddling clothes at Migdal Eder.

Luke 2:1 -7 "And it occurred in those days, that there headed out a mandate from Caesar Augustus, that all the world ought to be strained. When Cyrenius was guv of Syria.), (And this straining was initially made And also all mosted likely to be exhausted, every one into his own city. And Joseph additionally increased from Galilee, out of the city of Nazareth, right into Judaea, unto the city of David, which is called Bethlehem;(since he was of your home and family tree of David:-RRB- To be tired with Mary his upheld wife, being excellent with kid. Therefore it was, that, while they existed, the days were completed that she must be delivered. And also she yielded her firstborn child, as well as wrapped him in swaddling garments, and also.

laid him in a manger; due to the fact that there was no area for them in the inn.".

He was born at Migdal Eder. The boy of David that was the splendor of his daddy's house had no inheritance that he might regulate, no, not also in the city of David. He had no buddy that would certainly suit his mom in her distress with lodging. Christ was birthed in an inn, to intimate that he entered the globe to sojourn right here for some time.

An inn receives all comers, therefore does Christ. He hangs out the banner of love for his indication, as well as whoever comes to him, he will, in no wise erupted. Yet, unlike inns, he invites those that come without money and price.

That He was birthed in a delay where pets remained; as is implied by the word equated as a manger, a location for lambs to stand to be feed. Due to the fact that there was no room in the inn, as well as no comforts, he was stocked a manger, rather than a cradle.

The word which we provide swaddling clothes stems from a word that symbolizes to rend or tear, and these infer that he was so far from having good child-bed bed linen, that his very swaddles were rough as well as torn. His being birthed in a secure and stocked a manger was a proof of the poverty of his moms and dads.

So it existed in the lowly secure, behind a village Inn, that the maker of the globe chose to enter the mankind as a defenseless child. God, the Son, dressed his beautiful glory in the dustcloths of human flesh so as to end up being the:.
John 1:29 "Lamb of God, which taketh away the sin of the globe.".
Paradise, Eternity Past.
In the foreknowledge of God, He recognized prior to He produced the world and all that remains in it that His treasured development, "guy," would certainly rebel against Him. He also understood that the only means He can redeem fallen male would certainly cost the life of His sinless only begotten Son. However, God still developed man in His image.
John 3:16 -18 "For God so liked the world, that he offered his only begotten Son, that whosoever believeth.

in him must not perish, but have long lasting life. For God sent out not his Son into the globe to condemn the world; yet that the globe with him may be saved. He that believeth on him is not condemned: but he that believeth not is condemned currently because he hath not counted on the name of the only begotten Son of God.".
Why would God allow His Son to die on a cruel cross for you and me? Since He loved us with the sort of love that compromises oneself for one more. Other halves are commanded to like their wives as Christ enjoyed the Church and also gave Himself for it.
Ephesians 2:4 "But God, that is rich in grace, for his great love where with he loved us,".
1 John 4:19 "We love him since he first loved us".
Since God liked us as well as "the earnings of sin is fatality," and only a sinless

guy might crave another, Jesus was birthed into our humanity. Being birthed as a powerless child, expanding as a youngster, developing as a teen and ministering as an adult He "remained in all points attracted like as we are, yet without sin.".

It is just via the shed blood of Jesus Christ that we are fixed up with God as well as have assured entryway into Heaven. That is an individual issue. You need to think that Jesus needed you, to pay the incomes of your wrongs.

John 4:10 "Herein is love, not that we liked God, however that he liked us, and sent his Son to be the propitiation for our transgressions.".

Job or No Vacancy.

Much has actually been composed and also preached regarding the innkeeper that had "No Room" for Jesus. Throughout the years he has actually been demonized and also maligned by several preachers as well as educators. Nonetheless, the Bible does not tell us that he.

was, the name of his establishment, how big it was or anything concerning him or his family. We do not know if he was kind or hoggish, secular or godly.

We just know that he assisted give a manger. An area where the guards can "discover the babe covered in swaddling garments, lying in a manger.".

The inquiry to you today is, do you have any room in your heart for Jesus? Or does your heart claim," NO VACANCY.".

Chapter Six
The Sign

As a youngster, I lived in Erie, Pennsylvania for a while. Because jobs were a lot more abundant in Erie than Altoona, my parents had moved us there on the referral of my uncle Bill. Grandmother as well as the rest of the family lived in Altoona. Several times a year my Mom and also Dad, Aunt as well as Uncle, 2 relatives and also I would certainly stack right into the family members cars and truck as well as head southern for a weekend see. It was generally a four-hour drive, each way.

Nonetheless, one Sunday mid-day as we headed residence, Uncle Bill, that later ended up being a Baltimore taxi driver, located a "faster way." The method we had been taking a trip for several trips was verified and also reliable. It was chosen by the grownups, to take the untried way. We transformed the journey right into a tough five as well as a half hour excursion with northwestern Pennsylvania. Sometimes the tried and tested means is the very best means.

The Bible records a comparable circumstance where the male of God recommended the king to trust fund God as He had actually constantly led Israel on the right course. But, King Ahaz assumed he understood better.

In 787 BC King Ahaz, of Judah, was confronted with one of the most stressful scenario in the history of Israel considering that King David had actually developed the Kingdom. As a result of his bad practices, praise of various other gods and also having actually compromised his son to the Canaanite gods; God permitted his kingdom ahead under the control of Tiglath-Pilneser, the king of Assyria.

Pekah, king of Ephraim and Rezin king of Syria, additionally lieges, outlined.

to rebel against Assyria as well as planned to take Jerusalem with them, also if they had to dominate Ahaz and also change him with a king of their picking. Into this circumstance, God sent out the prophet Isaiah. Isaiah warned Ahaz not to become associated with the conspiracy. To persuade Ahaz to count on the God of Israel, Isaiah informed him to request a sign from God, "ask it either in the deepness or in the height over." If God met the indication asked for, Ahaz was after that in the setting of the of needing to rely on the Lord God for his delivery and not his management.

Ahaz, reduced in the Bible tale, from Jehoahaz, meaning Jehovah hath confiscated, probably indicating his spiritual condition due to his abhorrent apostasy. To trust Jehovah would certainly indicate giving up his prayer of the Baal gods and his evil way of living. Ahaz, therefore, refused to believe God for delivery.

Ahaz stripped the Temple treasury of its gold and silver and also sent it to Assyria in a vain attempt to employ their aid versus the accomplices. Therefore, Syria as well as Ephraim eliminated thousands of thousands of Judah's soldiers and took lots of slaves. He was additionally, attacked by the Edomites and also the Philistines. The Assyrians took the wealth of Israel and

also did not send or offer help.
II Chron. 28:19 -20 "For the Lord brought Judah low as a result of Ahaz, king of Israel; for he made Judah naked, and also oversteped sore versus the Lord. As well as Tiglath-Pilneser, king of Assyria came unto him and also troubled him, yet enhanced him not.".
Ahaz lost all around.
Nonetheless, God picked this context to reveal His first prophetic statement of Emmanuel coming to save. Ahazhad refused to recognize God. God refused to assist Israel's evil king, Ahaz.
God after that turned His interest to the country of Israel as well as informed them exactly how to recognize the good king that would certainly come.

Isaiah 7:14 "Therefore the Lord Himself shall offer you an indicator; Behold a virgin shall develop and birth a son, and shall call his name Immanuel.".
Israel had a wicked king and also needed to find out about the assured Messiah. 8 centuries later on a team of guards, were seeing their flocks when the angel of the Lord showed up and also told them the Christ is born.
Luke 2:12 "And this shall be an indication unto you; Ye will find the infant, wrapped in swaddling clothing, lying in a manger.".
The "indication" promised to Israel in Ahaz's day was the Saviour as well as Messiah that the shepherds experienced that evening in Bethlehem. It is fascinating that the gratification of Isaiah's prophecy was not to the leaders or the spiritual leaders, yet to the ordinary people. The guards were looking for the Christ, while their leaders had no area for the Saviour. God had sent His Son to redeem the world as well as pay the wrong financial obligation for humankind, and also almost every person missed His coming. Thirty-two years

later on, nationwide Israel declined God's king and also tortured their Saviour. Since the day Christ died, God has relied on the Gentiles to construct His Church and evangelize the globe, until the moment Israel will repent.
Matthew 16:13 -18 "When Jesus entered the coasts of Caesarea Philippi, he asked his adherents, stating, Whom do guys claim that I the Son of male am? As well as they stated Some say that thou art John the Baptist: some, Elias; as well as others, Jeremias, or among the prophets. He saith unto them, But whom say ye that I am? And also Simon Peter answered as well as said, Thou art the Christ, the Son of the living God. As well as Jesus answered as well as stated unto him, Blessed art thou, Simon Barjona: for flesh as well as blood hath not.

disclosed it unto thee, but my Father which remains in paradise. As well as I say also unto thee, That thou art Peter, and upon this rock, I will build my church; and also the gates of hell shall not dominate against it.".
Jesus built His Church upon Peter's sincere declaration "Thou art the Christ, the Son of the living God." Jesus, the Messiah, as well as Saviour pertained to conserve us from our transgressions that evening at Migdal Eder in Bethlehem. Though repetitively prophesied in the Old Testament, extremely few were looking for His coming.
Points have not altered in 2 thousand years. This same Jesus, that rejected in 32 AD is returning. This time around not as a babe yet, as the King. Not as a Saviour however as a conqueror. Not to bow down, but to be acquiesced as Lord and King.
Isaiah 45:20 -25 "Come and put together yourselves; draw near with each other, ye that are escaped of the countries: they have no expertise that established the timber of their graven picture, and pray unto a god that can not

conserve. Tell ye, and also bring them near; yea, let them take counsel together: that hath declared this from old time? Who hath told it from that time? Have not I the LORD? And also there is no God else beside me; a simply God and also a Saviour; there is none close to me. Look unto me, as well as be ye conserved, all the ends of the planet: for I am God, as well as there is none else. I have actually advocated myself, words is gone out of my mouth in nonpartisanship, and will not return, That unto me every knee will bow, every tongue will promise. Definitely, shall one claim, in the LORD have I sanctity as well as stamina: even to him shall males.

come; and all that are incensed against him will repent. In the LORD shall all the seed of Israel be justified, and also shall glory.".

Romans 14:11 -12 "For it is created, As I live, saith the Lord, every knee will bow to me, and also every tongue will confess to God. So then each people shall dictate, of himself, to God.".

Soon Jesus will certainly remove His church as well as establish His kingdom, established things right, and rule in perfect tranquility for one thousand years.

Luke 21:26 -28 "Men's hearts failing them for concern, and also for caring for those points which are beginning the earth: for the powers of paradise shall be trembled. And afterwards will they see the Son of man coming in a cloud with power and terrific splendor. And when these points begin to find to pass, then search for, as well as lift up your heads; for your redemption draweth nigh.".

Are you looking for Him?

Chapter Seven
The Greatest Gift

I got back one evening annoyed and also tired, as well as there it remained in the middle of the living room floor. "What's that," I asked my better half.
" I don't know. Your daddy dropped it off for you," She replied.
" But why?It's not my birthday or Christmas. It's not our Anniversary

is it?"

" No dear, he just stated that you needed it right now."
Inside package was Dad's one and only Magna-Cleaner. The just one

in existence. Dad made it several years back. In some way he recognized that I needed it to clean-up our flood-stained personal belongings before they entered our new house. I had actually invested a great deal of time trying to find a substitute so I might complete this task. My father had one, but we weren't talking. I thought I could do it myself anyhow. You know 'My method.' However, now with his wonderful present, I was ready to remove the discolorations and also relocate right into my brand-new residence, as well as it would be ideal.
A hunch, my papa's a great deal like our God.
We spend our time searching for a method to clean-up our lives and await a home in Heaven. We try doing kindness, saying petitions as well as just being as righteous as we can. We recognize it isn't good sufficient to please a Holy

God, and also make Him desire us to live with Him in Glory.
John 3:16 "For God so loved the world, that he gavehisonlybegottenSon, thatwhosoever.

believeth in him must not die, yet have eternal life.".
Virtually, 2,000 years ago God made a way that we can go into Heaven and have eternal life. He offered His only Son to pass away on Calvary for you as well as me. This gracious gift of his Son cleanses us from the spots of wrong and also makes us acceptable to God. When we required Him and did what we might not do for ourselves, he came simply.
Isaiah 64:6 "But we are all as a dirty point, as well as all our sanctities are as gross dustcloths ...".
Our goodness is to God as filthy cloths. Even our finest compared to God's Holiness is only garbage. Our Heavenly Father made provision for us.
1 John 1:9 "If we confess our sins, he is loyal as well as simply to forgive us our wrongs, and also to clean us from all unrighteousness.".
We stand prior to God as condemned to spend an infinity in Hell. Our transgression has made us guilty before God.
John 3:18 "He that believeth on him is not condemned: but he that believeth not is condemned currently because he hath not relied on the name of the only begotten Son of God.".
God provided us the present of His only excellent and also sinless kid, that passed away in our place. God sent His kid to conserve us from the fine of our transgressions as well as offer us immortality with Him in heaven.
John 3:17 "For God sent not his Son right into the globe to condemn the world; however that the world through him may be saved.".
What a wonderful gift! I could never ever provide one of my children to conserve even a great man. However, God liked us sufficient to offer His Only Son to crave.

us. Incredible love, just how can it be. I do not understand it, yet I rejoice God does. Currently we can stand before God as Just. Ask Him to save you, and also God will give you the gift of His Son, as Saviour from the charge of sin. Romans 5:7 -8 "For rarely for a righteous guy will certainly one die: yet peradventure for a good male some would certainly even dare to pass away. God commendeth his love toward us, in that, while we were yet sinners, Christ passed away for us.".

Chapter Eight
Wise Men Still Seek Him

It felt excellent, lastly, to set down on something that had not been always relocating. The smart men's lengthy trip currently practically ended, as well as dirty and also however tired the tourists beinged in the outer court waiting to see the king. After an impatient delay that appeared as lengthy as the journey itself, the word came that King Herod would see them now.

" Greetings gents, what is the function of your see? You should be tired" talked Herod the Great as they entered his large throne room.

" Congratulations King Herod, we have actually come to see your child. As well as to worship Him.".

" My boy?" Herod questioned.

" Yes, we are right here to see the newborn King and to worship before Him," stated Gaspar. "We have actually traveled over a thousand miles of warm desert to bless your kid.".

Herod rather puzzled described to the site visitors that he had no newborn son. Then he asked them what triggered them to take a trip completely from Persia to Jerusalem. The Magi informed Herod that for generations their Grandfathers as well as papas had been researching the scrolls offered Babylon by the prophets when Nebuchadnezzar took them hostage. Their forefathers had been the sensible guys of Babylon. The ones Daniel had rescued from death and also educated them the Holy Scriptures. For centuries they had actually been examining these works and when the star appeared they understood that God had sent His Messiah. They packed their caravan as well as came to see this fantastic.

prophetic satisfaction.
" Star, what star?" asked Herod.
" The star stated by the prophet Moses as tape-recorded in Numbers.".
Numbers 24:17 "I will see him, yet not currently: I will behold him, yet not nigh: there will come a Star out of Jacob, as well as a Sceptre shall climb out of Israel, and also shall smite the corners of Moab, and also destroy all the youngsters of Sheth.".
" When we saw His celebrity we concerned the royal residence to see the newborn king," they responded. "Where would certainly you anticipate to locate the King of the Jews, but in the palace at Jerusalem?".
They likewise possibly had examined the prophecy of Daniel worrying the resulting the Messiah.
Daniel 9:23 -25 "... as a result recognize the issue, and also take into consideration the vision. Seventy weeks are established upon thy people and upon thy divine city, to end up the transgression, and also to make an end of wrongs, as well as to make reconciliation for iniquity, and also to bring in eternal nonpartisanship, and to secure up the vision and prediction, and also to bless one of the most Holy. Know for that reason and recognize, that from the going forth of the commandment to bring back and also to develop Jerusalem

unto the Messiah the Prince shall be seven weeks, as well as threescore and 2 weeks: ...".
Herod ensured them that there was no king in Judah other than him, Herod the Great, as assigned by the Roman Senate. After that Herod had a suggestion as well as called the scribes. They were the keepers of the Law, Prophets, and History. It would certainly be in the wisdom of the scribes if anybody can fix this matter.

When they arrived, Herod asked "Where Christ should be birthed?".
While the scribes looked for a response to the king's concern, Herod pressed the wise men to learn more on when the star appeared, as well as how much time they had actually been taking a trip.
After a quick trip to the Temple, perhaps to see Simeon, the old guy who understood about that stuff or to speak with others the scribes went back to the royal residence with the news that the Christ would be birthed in Bethlehem as was written by the prophet Micah.
Micah 5:2 "But thou, Bethlehem Ephratah, though thou be little amongst the thousands of Judah, yet out of thee will he emerge unto me that is to be ruler in Israel; whose goings forth have been from of old, from eternal.".
" I believed for a minute that we were misinterpreted. Yet, we only missed our destination by 5 miles. Let us go bros as well as look for Him in Bethlehem."
"We should have recognized to look in the city of David's lineage.".
They quickly covered this last brief range as well as assisted by His star located your house where the kid was. Once they went into the home of Joseph as well as Mary and saw the child, they recognized that their trip had ended successfully. Definitely this Jesus was Immanuel, God with us. After providing

their presents of gold for His nobility, Frankincense for His pureness and Myrrh for His death and funeral the smart males knelt and also worshiped their Messiah, thanking as well as commending Yahweh for sending His Son. They departed to relax from the activities of this most interesting day when they had completed.

Next morning as they each prepared their camels for the return journey they discovered that each had actually had a dream in the night. Every one had the same desire. An Angel informed them not to return to Herod, for he sought to harm the kid and not to prayer him as he had actually said. They departed for Persia an additional method.

It has been almost 2 thousand years since that occurrence happened. Things have not transformed a lot. Outside of a couple of guards, some typical folk as well as these smart guys, no person was seeking for the Saviour. Today, the.

political leaders and also leaders of this world seek only to raise their power and authority. They aren't seeking the Christ. The 'religious' simply pay Him lip service. They build grand as well as complex 'Good Works' systems to get support with God. They are as well active with their programs to seek the Saviour. The merchants press His birthday, starting in October, however, only commercial.

Isaiah 56:11 -12 "Yea, they are greedy pet dogs which can never ever have enough, and they are guards that can not comprehend: they all want to their very own way, each for his gain, from his quarter. Come ye, state they, I will certainly fetch wine, as well as we will fill ourselves with solid drink; as well as tomorrow will be as this particular day, as well as a lot more plentiful.".

And also, oh yes, a few sensible men still seek Him.

Chapter Nine
The Wait is Over

" Wake-up my wonderful Mary, you require to registered nurse the child and prepare for His meeting with the Priest. We must fulfill our obligation to Jehovah.".

Luke 2:21 "And when eight days were accomplished for the circumcising of the youngster, his name was called JESUS, which was so named of the angel prior to he was developed in the womb.".

Jesus was born into a very Jewish household which kept all the Jewish laws blamelessly. Jesus involved satisfy the law. Paul remarked:.

Galatians 4:4 "But when the fulness of the time was come, God sent out forth his Son, made of a female, made under the law.".

The eighth day after birth represents putting the sign of the Covenant upon each male child that becomes part of the country of Israel.

Genesis 17:10 -14 "This is my agreement, which ye will maintain, in between me and also you and thy seed after thee; Every male child amongst you will be circumcised. As well as ye shall circumcise the flesh of your foreskin; and it will be a token of the covenant between me as well as you. And also he that is.

eight days old shall be circumcised amongst you, every guy kid in your generations, he that is born in your house, or bought with cash of any unfamiliar person, which is not of thy seed. He that is born in thy house, and also he that is gotten with thy cash, should needs be circumcised: as well as my agreement shall be in your flesh for an eternal covenant. And the uncircumcised man kid whose flesh of his foreskin is not circumcised, that heart shall be removed from his people; he hath busted my commitment.".
Leviticus 12:1 -3 "And the LORD spake unto Moses, saying, Speak unto the children of Israel, saying, If a lady have conceived seed, as well as birthed a male child: then she will be unclean 7 days; according to the days of the splitting up for her infirmity will she be dirty. As well as in the 8th day the flesh of his foreskin shall be circumcised.".

At His Circumcision, He received the name Jesus as was the guideline of the Angel to Joseph, the earthly head of the family members.
Matthew 1:20 -21 "... the angel of the Lord appeared unto him in a dream, claiming, Joseph, thou son of David, fear not to take unto thee Mary thy spouse: for that which is developed in her is of the Holy Ghost. As well as she will come up with a child, as well as thou shalt call his name JESUS: for he shall conserve his people from their sins.".
Thirty-three days later, Joseph once again hurried Mary for one more conference with the Temple Priest. Today she would provide the sacrifice called for because.

of her having brought to life a kid.
Leviticus 12:2 -8 "Speak unto the youngsters of Israel, claiming, if a lady have actually developed seed, and born a male youngster: after that she will be unclean 7 days; according to the days of the splitting up for her infirmity will she be dirty. And in the 8th day, the flesh of his foreskin shall be circumcised. As well as she shall after that proceed in the blood of her purifying three and thirty days; she shall touch no solemn point, neither enter the sanctuary, till the days of her purifying be fulfilled. But if she bear a maid child, after that she will be unclean 2 weeks, as in her separation: as well as she shall continue in the blood of her purifying threescore and six days. And when the days of her purifying are fulfilled, for a boy, or for a daughter, she will bring a lamb of the first year for a burnt offering, and also a young pigeon, or a turtledove, for a wrong offering, unto the door of the habitation of the churchgoers, unto the priest: Who shall supply it prior to the LORD, and also make a satisfaction for her; and she will be cleaned from the issue of her blood. This is the regulation for her that have actually born a male or a female. And also if she be unable to bring a lamb, then she will bring two turtles, or more young pigeons; the one for the burned offering, and the other for a transgression offering: and also the clergyman will make an atonement for her, and she will be tidy.".
Joseph prepared the little sacrifice needed by legislation, and as they were.

in deep hardship and far from house they might not afford a lamb They brought 2 little birds as an offering for her purification. The sacrifice for her cleansing needed an offering on a fortieth day at the Nicanor Gate on the east of the Court of Women.

Luke 2:22 -24 "And when the days of her purification according to the regulation of Moses were completed, they brought him to Jerusalem, to present him to the Lord; (As it is created in the legislation of the Lord, Every man that openeth the womb shall be called divine to the Lord;-RRB- And to use a sacrifice according to that which is stated in the legislation of the Lord, A set of turtledoves, or 2 young pigeons.".

The very early Hebrews thought God's regulation:.

" Sanctify unto me all the firstborn, whatsoever openeth the womb amongst the kids of Israel, both of male as well as of monster: it is mine" Exodus 13:2.

They were "consecrated" or Holy" to God. While there, they met two elderly saints who had been seeking the coming Messiah.

" The event," says Edersheim, "consisted of the official discussion of the kid to the clergyman, accompanied by two brief orisons.

-- the very first one for the law of redemption, the other for the present of a firstborn boy, after which the redemption money was paid.".

Not mentioned in this account is the 'redemption' cash. Jesus is hence presented similarly as Samuel existed in the Old Testament, the redemption price to be paid by Himself on the Cross. Hannah's words, "So currently I give him to the Lord. For his entire life, he will certainly be given over to the Lord" 1 Samuel 1:28.

Luke 2:25 -32 "And, lay eyes on, there was a man in.

Jerusalem, whose name was Simeon; and the same man was simply and also sincere, waiting on the consolation of Israel: and the Holy Ghost was upon him. And it was revealed unto him by the Holy Ghost, that he should not see fatality prior to he had actually seen the Lord's, Christ. And also he came by the Spirit right into the temple: and also when the moms and dads brought in the kid Jesus, to do for him after the custom of the law, after that took he him up in his arms, and blessed God, and claimed, Lord, currently lettest thou thy servant depart in tranquility, according to thy word: For my own eyes have seen thy redemption, which thou hast prepared before the face of all individuals; A light to lighten the Gentiles as well as the glory of thy individuals Israel.

Simeon is a Hebrew name, which implies "hearing" in Hebrew. He was, unquestionably listening to the Holy Spirit's guarantees and also direction. Simeon has been eagerly anticipating to see the Messiah. It is not unintended that Jesus' name, in Hebrew Yeshua, implies literally, "salvation." So Simeon searches the child called "Salvation" and also claims, "my eyes have actually seen your salvation ...".

God sent His boy, birthed of a virgin to save us from our sins. Simeon sees Jesus' salvation as encompassing all individuals-- Gentiles and also Jews alike. Isaiah 49:6 "And he said, It is a light thing that thou shouldest be my servant to raise up the tribes of Jacob, and to restore the preserved of Israel: I will certainly likewise provide thee for a light to the Gentiles, that thou mayest be my salvation unto completion of the planet.".

Simeon prophesies to Mary the future of humankind. Just how people reply to

Jesus and also His message will certainly determine their everlasting destiny. Think on the Lord Jesus Christ as well as be conserved or do not believe and continue to be.

condemned. Jesus is God's sign to his people, yet He will certainly be declined. Simeon can see the deep suffering that Mary will certainly really feel as her son is rejected by the country's religious leaders and also ultimately tortured. Luke 2:33 -35 "And Joseph as well as his mommy marveled at those things which were spoken of him. And also Simeon blessed them, and also said unto Mary his mom, Behold, this youngster is established for the loss and also climbing again of lots of in Israel; as well as for an indication which will be spoken against; (Yea, a sword will puncture via thy own heart likewise,) that the ideas of several hearts might be exposed.".

Next off, they satisfy Anna, an 84-year-old woman, that is a pious slave in the Woman's Court of the Temple.

Luke 2:21 -40 "And there was one Anna, a prophetess, the daughter of Phanuel, of the tribe of Aser: she was of an excellent age, as well as had lived with a partner seven years from her virginity; And she was a widow of about fourscore and 4 years, which departed not from the holy place, yet offered God with fasting's as well as prayers night and day. As well as she being available in that immediate gave thanks likewise unto the Lord, and spake of him to all them that looked for redemption in Jerusalem. As well as when they had actually done all points according to the legislation of the Lord, they returned into Galilee, to their very own city Nazareth. And also the kid grew, and waxed strong in spirit, filled with wisdom: and also the poise of God was upon him.". Dr. Ralph F. Wilson writes "Can't you see her? An old lady, a widow.

for numerous, years, with absolutely nothing to do yet to praise. Therefore she does. She virtually lives in the Women's Court of the Temple, night and day. As well as she is a prophetess, a female prophet.".

Anna gives thanks to God for sending out the redemption of Jerusalem. When Jerusalem will when again be free from Roman injustice, the time. After meeting the obligations of the Law of Moses, Joseph, Mary and also the baby Jesus mosted likely to Egypt, as advised by the angel.

Matthew 2:13 -23 "And when they were left, lay eyes on, the angel of the Lord appeareth to Joseph in a desire, stating, Arise, and take the child and his mom, and leave right into Egypt, and also be thou there up until I bring thee word: for Herod will certainly seek the kid to damage him. When he occurred, he took the young child and his mommy by evening, and departed into Egypt: And was there till the fatality of Herod: that it might be satisfied which was spoken of the Lord by the prophet, claiming, Out of Egypt have I called my kid. After that Herod, when he saw that he was mocked of the sensible guys, was exceeding wroth, as well as sent forth, as well as multitude all the kids that were in Bethlehem, as well as in all the shores thereof, from 2 years of ages and under, according to the moment which he had actually diligently asked of the sensible males. After that was met that which was spoken by Jeremy the prophet, saying, In Rama existed a voice heard, lamentation, and also weeping, and also excellent mourning, Rachel weeping for her kids, and would not be comforted, since they are not. When Herod was dead, lay eyes on, an angel of the Lord.

appeareth in a dream to Joseph in Egypt, Saying, Arise, as well as take the kid and also his mommy, and enter into the land of Israel: for they are dead which looked for the young child's life. And also he developed, and took the young child and his mommy, as well as came into the land of Israel. When he heard that Archelaus did rule in Judaea in the area of his father Herod, he was terrified to go thither: not-withstanding, being warned of God in a dream, he transformed apart into the components of Galilee: And he came as well as dwelt in a city called Nazareth: that it might be met which was spoken by the prophets, He will be called a Nazarene.".
After the fatality of Herod, and also as advised by an angel Joseph as well as Mary went back to Galilee, and also to their city Nazareth.

Chapter Ten
His Name Is

The Christmas song goes "Jesus, Jesus, Jesus, There's something about that name"

> *Luke 2:30-33 "And the angel said unto her, Fear not, Mary: for thou hast found favour with God. And, behold, thou shalt conceive in thy womb and bring forth a son, and shalt call his name JESUS. He shall be great, and shall be called the Son of the Highest: and the Lord God shall give unto him the throne of his father David: And he shall reign over the house of Jacob forever, and of his kingdom, there shall be no end."*

His name "Jesus" (Hebrew *Yeshua*) means, "salvation."

To Adam God was known as Almighty God and Creator.

> *Genesis 1:1 "In the beginning, God created the heaven and the earth."*

God is Supreme – All Power All-Knowing, Always Presence.

God is Sovereign – He can do whatever He wants when He wants.

Adam, Seth, Enos, Cainan, Mahalaleel, Enoch, Methuselah, Noah, Shem, Abraham, Isaac Jacob and the Israelites of Egypt all knew God as Elohim, *God Almighty, Creator*

After 2000 years God revealed His name to Moses as *Yahweh, I AM.* Eternal Presence.

> *Exodus 3:13 "And Moses said unto God, Behold, when I come unto the children of Israel, and shall say unto them, The God of your fathers hath sent me unto you; and they shall say to me, what is his name? what shall I say unto them? [14]And God said unto Moses; I AM THAT I AM: and he said, thus shalt thou say unto the children of Israel, I AM hath sent me unto you."*

In the Midrash, the Hebrew scholars explain this as an active manifestation of the divine existence. God is active in the affairs of His world and His people. The Midrash states: "Although He has not displayed His power towards you, He will do so. He is eternal and will certainly redeem you."

> *Exodus 3:15 "And God said moreover unto Moses, thus shalt thou say unto the children of Israel, The LORD God of your fathers, the God of Abraham, the God of Isaac, and the God of Jacob, hath sent me unto you: this is my name for ever, and this is my memorial unto all generations."*

LORD, here is the translation of the Divine Name written in four Hebrew letters *YHWH* . A name, so holy that the Hebrew scribes would not speak it or write it without first cleansing themselves.

It gives expression to the fact that He was, He is and that He will be forever. This name also stresses the loving-kindness and faithfulness of GOD unto His creatures.

> *Exodus 6:2 "And God spake unto Moses, and said unto him, I am the LORD And I appeared unto Abraham, unto Isaac, and unto Jacob, by*

the name of God Almighty (Elohim), but by my name JEHOVAH (Yahweh) was I not known to them."

From Strong's Concordance*; (the) self-Existent or Eternal*; *Jehovah*, Jewish national name of God: —Jehovah, the Lord.

God revealed another name to Moses during a war with Amalek, Joshua fought. Aaron & Hur supported Moses' arms.

Exodus 17:13-16 "And Joshua discomfited Amalek and his people with the edge of the sword. And the LORD said unto Moses, Write this for a memorial in a book, and rehearse it in the ears of Joshua: for I will utterly put out the remembrance of Amalek from under heaven. And Moses built an altar, and called the name of it Jehovahnissi: For he said Because the LORD hath sworn that the LORD will have war with Amalek from generation to generation."

Jehovahnissi; translates to Jehovah (is) my banner; *Jehovah-Nissi*, is also a symbolical name of an altar in the Sinai Desert.

To Gideon, He revealed himself as Jehovah-Salom.

Judges 6:11-12 "And there came an angel of the LORD, and sat under an oak which was in Ophrah, that pertained unto Joash the Abiezrite: and his son Gideon threshed wheat by the winepress, to hide it from the Midianites. And the angel of the LORD appeared unto him, and said unto him; The LORD is with thee, thou mighty man of valour."

When Gideon is cowering behind the winepress threshing wheat in secret, God revealed Himself to Gideon by consuming the sacrifice with fire, as the God of who would bring peace to Israel. Gideon named the place

Jehovah-Shalom.

> *Judges 6:23-24 "And the LORD said unto him; Peace be unto thee; fear not: thou shalt not die. Then Gideon built an altar there unto the LORD, and called it Jehovahshalom: unto this day it is yet in Ophrah of the Abiezrites."*

Jehovah (is) *peace*; *Jehovah-Shalom*, a symbolical name of an altar in Palestine.

Throughout the Old Testament He revealed other attributes in His names:

Jehovah Rofi - The God who heals

Jehovah Jireh – The God who supplies

Jehovah Tsidkenu – The God of my righteousness

Jehovah Shammah – The God who is thither.

To the nation of Israel in Ahaz 'day, God revealed Himself as Immanuel.

> *Isaiah 7:14 "Therefore the Lord himself shall give you a sign; Behold, a virgin shall conceive, and bear a son, and shall call his name Immanuel."*

Immanuel means; *with us (is) God;*

God has a desire to dwell with humanity as he did in the garden.

> *Genesis 3:8-9 "And they heard the voice of the LORD God walking in the garden in the cool of the day: and Adam and his wife hid themselves from the presence of the LORD God amongst the trees of the garden. And the LORD God called unto Adam, and said unto him, Where art thou?"*

But Mary was told to call His name *JESUS.*

> *Luke 1:31 "...And, behold, thou shalt conceive in thy womb, and bring forth a son, and shalt call his name JESUS"*

Jehovah-saved; *Jehoshua* (that is, Joshua), the Jewish leader: —Jehoshua, Jehoshuah, Joshua, Jesus in the New Testament Greek.

Joseph was also told in a dream from God to name Him *JESUS.*

> *Mark 1:20-25 "But while he thought on these things, behold, the angel of the Lord appeared unto him in a dream, saying, Joseph, thou son of*

David, fear not to take unto thee Mary thy wife: for that which is conceived in her is of the Holy Ghost. And she shall bring forth a son, and thou shalt call his name JESUS: for he shall save his people from their sins. Now all this was done, that it might be fulfilled which was spoken of the Lord by the prophet, saying, Behold, a virgin shall be with child, and shall bring forth a son, and they shall call his name Emmanuel, which being interpreted is, God with us. Then Joseph being raised from sleep did as the angel of the Lord had bidden him, and took unto him his wife: [25]And knew her not till she had brought forth her firstborn son: and he called his name JESUS."

Of Hebrew origin, *Jehoshua*, the name of our Lord and two (three) other Israelites: translates *JESUS* .

God came to save us:

Jesus the Elohim, I AM, YHWH, and Jehovah of the Old Testament willingly cloaked His glory and majesty in the small body of an infant and became Emmanuel. So he could have all the temptations and trials that we have and yet live a sinless life. The last half of Luke chapter two talks about what happened when Jesus was;

Eight days old (verse 21);

Forty days old (verse 22-38);

During His childhood (verse 39-40);

Twelve years old (verse 41-50);

A young adult (verse 51-52).

That last verse—Luke 2:52—is our goal for our children—that they will mature as He did: mentally (in wisdom), physically (in stature), spiritually (in favor with God), and socially (and men).

So he could fulfill His name:

"Jesus, Jesus, Jesus
There is something about that name."

JESUS SAVES

Chapter Eleven
Born to Die

When a son is born into a family, especially a firstborn son, there is a great joy for the whole family. Someone to keep the family name going for another generation. Someone to be added to the business name "and Son." The new parents have great plans for their offspring. He will be a star athlete or a great warrior or a Senator, Judge or even the President of the United States. The potential for the new baby is unlimited. Then we also think of the beautiful Grandchildren that they will produce.

All children are born with the expectation of long and fruitful lives. All that is, but one. Jesus was born into our world with the expressed purpose of dying in payment of our sin debt to God.

> *John 3:16 "For God so loved the world, that he gave his only begotten Son, that whosoever believeth in him should not perish, but have everlasting life."*

God, in the person of Jesus, the Son of God created a perfect world. In Genesis three, Adam and Eve disobeyed God by taking of the forbidden fruit. Thus sin entered into God's perfect world. From that one act of rebellion, the sin nature of man's parents passed to every human ever born. We all have sinned.

> *Romans 3:23 "For all have sinned, and come short of the glory of God;"*

The glory of God requires us to be perfect, sinless and believing his Word. To be accepted by a Holy God, you must be holy. Any sin or flaw disqualifies us with God and earns us His judgment. You, I and Everyone else are sinners. That was settled when you raided the cookie jar after mom said "no." It sounds cruel, but it only takes one little mark to ruin perfection. God created a perfect world, without sickness of death and Adam's sin allowed a flaw to enter God's perfect world and corrupt it. You do not have to teach a child to do bad things. The sin nature in already inbred.

> *Romans 6:23 "For the wages of sin is death; but the gift of God is eternal life through Jesus Christ our Lord."*

Wages are what we earn for the work that we perform. Death is the payment we receive for the sins we have committed against God. So since sin causes both physical and spiritual death God provided a plan to rescue man from the eternal death. We will all face physical death, except for a few who are caught up to be with Jesus when he returns. I wrote about that in my book "Look Up: Redemption in this Generation." For everyone else:

> *Hebrews 9:27 "It is appointed unto men once to die but after this the judgment."*

So God made a way by using an innocent, sinless substitute. When Adam and Eve sinned, God used the blood of an animal to cover their sin and the animal skins to cover their shame. That set the standard for meeting God's requirements until he sent Jesus, the sinless Lamb of God to be our Substitute.

This was the will of God the Father, and Jesus was willing to be the sacrifice.

> *John 5:30 "I can of mine own self, do nothing: as I hear, I judge: and my judgment is just; because I seek not mine own will, but the will of the Father which hath sent me."*

> *John 4:34 "Jesus saith unto them, My meat is to*

do the will of him that sent me and to finish his work."

Jesus came, to die because He loved us.

John 15:13 "Greater love hath no man than this that a man lay down his life for his friends."

Romans 10:9-10 "That if thou shalt confess with thy mouth the Lord Jesus, and shalt believe in thine heart that God hath raised him from the dead, thou shalt be saved. For with the heart man believeth unto righteousness, and with the mouth confession is made unto salvation."

Romans 10:13 "For whosoever shall call upon the name of the Lord shall be saved."

Just believe that Jesus paid the price for your sins and you will be saved from the wrath of a Holy God. It's that simple. It's that easy.

John 1:12 "...many as received him, to them gave he power to become the sons of God, even to them that believe on his name:"

He sent His Son so that we might be saved from God's wrath and have eternal life with Jesus in heaven.

Bibliography

airchild, Mary, Meet Mary: the Mother of Jesus. Thought Co. 2017

ockyer, Herbert, All the Women of the Bible, Grand Rapids MI: Lamplighter Books,

Mcgee, J. Vernon, Daniel. Nashville, TN. Thomas Nelson Publishing 1991

entecost, J. Dwight, The Words and Works of Jesus Christ. Grand Rapids, MI: Academie Books, 1981

ice, John R. *King of the Jews.* Murfreesboro, TN: Sword of the Lord Publishers, 1955

ice, John R. *The Son of Man.* Murfreesboro, TN: Sword of the Lord Publishers, 1971

eigler, James D, Thoughts of Christmas, Lake Monticello, VA: Jim Zeigler Writings, 2007

her Books and Writings by Jim Zeigler

Books:

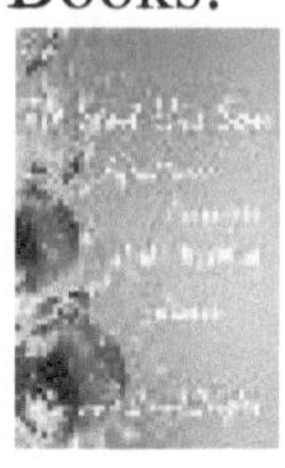
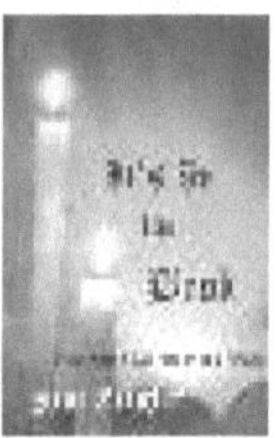

Look Up: Redemption in this Generation		2016
He Sent His Son	Sept	2017
It's in the Book		2018

Writings:

Mommy, I Love You

Hey Dad

America, Prepare to meet thy God The

Last Blood

The Visit

In the Gap

Another Watereth

www.ingramcontent.com/pod-product-compliance
Lightning Source LLC
LaVergne TN
LVHW040917150826
845672LV00007B/2089

* 9 7 9 8 7 5 5 9 0 2 4 3 4 *